Stepping Stones

by

Patti Sparrow

A collection of inspirational quotes and affirmations, for a world in need of more love.

Photography by

Kathleen Warren

Stepping Stones © Patti Sparrow and Kathleen Warren

Published by Nature Woman Wisdom

First Edition. Printed and bound in the United States of America. All rights reserved. No part of this book may be reproduced in any form or by any electronic or mechanical means, including information storage and retrieval systems, recording, or photocopying, without permission in writing from the publisher, except by a reviewer, who may quote brief passages in review or where permitted by law.

Copyright © 2012 Patti Sparrow and Kathleen Warren

ISBN-13:
978-0615653280 (Nature Woman Wisdom)

ISBN-10:
0615653286
Printed in The United States of America

June 2012

10 9 8 7 6 5 4 3 2

Library of Congress Cataloging in Publication Data

Sparrow, Patti
   Stepping Stones

Meditation
   Patti Sparrow
   Stepping Stones

1.

This book is dedicated to the many people I know who have said they want to meditate but don't have the time for it in their hectic lives.

It is 31 of my favorite quotes, one for every day of the month. They are combined with short reflections on each.

I am grateful for the wisdom of these many teachers and sages, and hope to honor their words, with my thoughts.

My sister Kath has a magical eye for capturing truth and beauty in her photographs. In true sisterly manner we combine our talents to share something wonderful with you.

Read one meditation every morning with your breakfast tea!

See how it applies to your life right now.

Carry the thought with you throughout the day as you would carry a lucky stone in your pocket.

I hope our "stepping stones" will help **you** on your life journey. Enjoy,

Patti

Stepping Stones" has been such a joy to work on with my sister and terrific friend. It is a project I had considered doing some time ago and did not have the confidence to tackle. Instead, we inspired each other during the process and completed this book. Thank you.

Photography fills my very soul. I see the divine in nature. The best explanation for my work is the name of my photography business: "Kalein". Kalein is taken from the word Kalon which means beauty, or a calling. It is my soul calling to me to fill it with beauty and to share it with others: that they may see what I see and feel. It is the wisdom of love nourishing my love, and creating bliss.

I find this calling fulfilled in photography, capturing the beauty of the earth, in its places, people, birds, and animals, and, course, the light, which we all are. I relive each minute when I revisit photos and even more so when I see them through Patti's words, that seem to capture and explain even deeper, the emotions that exist in a captured moment.

Enjoy this lovely book. I wish for you to experience the bliss, peace and joy I have experienced and captured in my photography, and feel it in Patti's beautiful and inspirational words.

Blessings,

Kathleen Warren

"Life's ups and downs provide windows of opportunity
to determine your value and goals.
Think of using all obstacles as stepping stones to build the life you want."
- Marsha Sinetar

Hiking through the hilly woods of New England is an adventure in traversing rocks and stones of all sizes and shapes.

If you cross a stream you are guaranteed to slip on the wet moss and probably get your feet stuck in the mud on the other side. At least I do!

It's exhilarating and exhausting but worth all the obstacles when you reach a clearing and stop to catch your breath – and see the colors and life and beauty all around you.

Take time today

to look at your life and congratulate yourself on the many rocks and muddy stretches you have conquered.

Each one has given you a glimpse of the power you have to overcome them all, and build the life you want.

"To be yourself in a world that is constantly trying to make you something else is the greatest accomplishment."

- *Ralph Waldo Emerson*

6.

We live in an anxiety ridden society. We are bombarded with drugs, pills and miracle cures for everything that is "wrong" with us.

We look to the masked faces of Hollywood stars and professional athletes, being told that they are the idols we want to emulate. But those masks dry up and crack, and we see multiple failed marriages, arrests and addictions.

All the "cures" that are offered are really the illness. Happiness and fulfillment will not be found in a perfect body, if it covers an empty soul.

Today, reassure yourself that you really don't need to be fixed!

Every human being is flawed in some way; we are not supposed to be perfect. You are wonderful just as you are, with gifts and talents that need to be shared.. Wipe off the silly masks.

You shouldn't cover up who you are. Instead, Be authentic. Be you.

"Far away in the sunshine are my highest aspirations.
I may not reach them, but I can look up and see the beauty,
Believe in them, and try to follow where they lead."
- Louisa May Alcott

Do you dream of something else you'd really like to do with your life? I think most of us do, but all the everyday bill paying and chores seem to keep those yearnings far away and unattainable.

 And then the night time comes, and with sleep those imaginings come to life in the subconscious. The possibilities are endless in dreams, and can always have a happy ending. The morning comes and you shake it off as just a silly or childish hope.

Just for today, ignore all the reasons you can't follow that wish and instead picture how your life could be if at all came true.

Find just one thing you can do to step closer to making it real and do it!

Savor that giddy feeling of accomplishment and believe in all your highest possibilities.

Keep looking up- Follow the beckoning- It can be yours. Believe.

"Spread love everywhere you go. Let no one ever come to you without leaving happier."

- Mother Teresa

This is such a simple thought and yet so profound- and sometimes so hard to do. It's easy to be pleasant to happy people, but what about those mean, greedy, nasty ones? They don't deserve our love, Or maybe they need it the most. Think of how good it feels when you just do the right thing.

-offer your seat to someone elderly on the train.

-Give to your favorite charity.

-Let the mom with the screaming baby ahead in the checkout line

Those acts connect you to the highest part of your being. The more often you do kind acts, the closer you stay to the divine.

Try today to let your generosity extend to the really unlovable people in your life.

Trying to forgive the people who have harmed you releases the hate that weighs down your soul. Forgiveness can fill you with a gentle sense of fullness and peace. Give yourself the gift of an open and loving heart. It doesn't matter if they deserve it or not-

You do.

"Always do what you are afraid to do."

Ralph Waldo Emerson

I spent a good part of my adult life afraid of everything-convinced that no matter what I did, it was never good enough.

In a crowded cloud filled sky I would have pictured myself as the wispy one- no substance- erased in no time by the wind.

Always present though was a yearning for a life that I believed really mattered. It was a faint glow that slowly grew to a fire within me- burning to be noticed.

I gradually began to face my fears, and as I did – they disappeared- not me!

Today, do one small thing you are afraid to do.

-Say no thank you to that committee that you really don't want to join.

-Introduce yourself to someone you'd like to know better.

- Sign up for a class that intrigues you.

Take another look at the wispy cloud and realize

That it has shaped into a dragon -

A magical being just waiting to unleash its mighty power.

"Through return to simple living comes control of desires.

In control of desires stillness is attained.

In stillness the world is restored."

Lao Tzu

14.

This is a picture of early morning on the lake at a tiny summer cottage that has been in our family for over 75 years.

There is no running water, no heat, no television, and not even a working stove. Days are spent swimming, cooking outdoors, playing cards, and taking long quiet rides in a kayak. Nights are circles around a campfire, telling stories, slapping mosquitoes, and roasting marshmallows.

It's perfect.

Vacations at the cottage offer the opportunity to live very simply. Without electronic entertainment there is the chance to look within,

Breathe, relax, and dream.

Make time today for a simple pleasure.

Go for a long walk and let the stillness surround you. Watch the sun in its journey across the sky, and let it take your worries along with it. Listen to the sounds of all the life nearby – the trees, the birds, the dogs barking in the distance.

Breathe, relax and dream.

Let your world be restored.

"*If I want to be accepted as I am, then I need to be willing to accept others as they are.*"

Louise L. Hay

16.

What do you see in this picture?

Some may see an ugly face and fear those teeth- a ferocious animal that is going to attack. But I have learned that my dog Maggie is gentle with children no matter how much she is squeezed. She is loyal and protective of my home and can always be counted on to make me smile, and feel loved- just as I am.

If today you see someone ugly, or fat, or dirty, or even mean looking,

try to look a little deeper.

Take time to realize that they have talents and beauty inside. It may not be obvious, but it is true that all living creatures are precious. You don't want to be judged by your flaws-

No one does.

Take another look and see someone who wants to be loved and appreciated-

The same as you and me.

"A woman is like a tea bag.

You never know how strong she is until she gets in hot water."

Eleanor Roosevelt

I love this quote because it helps to see the possible positive in any uncomfortable situation. Oh yes- we do get ourselves into hot water-with actions, words or sometimes just bad luck. There have been many times that I have wished I could go back in time. If only I could change those unkind words or go back and make the right choice. Unfortunately that is not possible. We just have to find a way to live with the choices we made. These dilemmas do give us the opportunity to admit to our errors and find a way to create a solution.

Today, take a breath and face that annoyance whispering in the back of your thoughts.

It is one of those dilemmas waiting for a better solution. Take an objective look at it and test your strength to see if maybe this time you can find the right answer. The experience is here to learn from.

Face it and come through stronger- And maybe a little wiser.

"Hope is the thing with feathers that perches in the soul, and sings the tunes without the words, and never stops at all."

Emily Dickenson

Ever stop and sit quietly outside and just listen? Birds are such happy creatures, singing just because another day has begun.

No worries about what problems may arise today-

Or guilt about what was done wrong yesterday.

Just delighted to be alive-

    Or maybe sharing with us –

    If we listen, hope, for our souls.

Today, listen to the music of nature around you.

Let the wild things show you how blissful it is just to be alive.

Catch their exuberance and find something in your life to sing about:

    And let the tune

    Perch in your soul.

"Nothing is predestined:

The obstacles of your past can become the gateways that lead to new beginnings."

Ralph Blum

Kath and I visited the rainbow bridge a few years ago, both in the midst of career changes and spiritual searching. We both experienced the power of this ancient gateway and realized that sometimes what seems impossible can be very real.

It is important to go to places that inspire you. Feel the awe in nature's beauty.

Open your soul to all that could be possible for you.

Today- recall a place that was magical to you as a child.

Remember the joy and peace you felt there- the endless imaginative possibilities it offered.

Let them fill you once more.

Let them inspire you again.

They can still be gateways to hope and change in your life.

"A hero is an ordinary individual who finds the strength to persevere and endure in spite of overwhelming obstacles."

Christopher Reeve

I was blessed to have such a hero in my life. Papa lived next door, and I was with him every day growing up.

He ran away from an abusive home when he was 14 and later went to war with no one caring if he came back.

Through faith, perseverance and a powerful belief in self-reliance, he married the girl of his dreams, worked through the depression when many did not, and raised a family of 6 children - 1 rescued from a childhood similar to his own.

An ordinary man,

A precious gift to me.

Today, think about, and thank, someone who has touched you with their life.

Whether they are alive or not, acknowledge their gift to you.

Think about who you may be inspiring with your life.

You can be a hero too.

"I am the gardener of my mind.
I remove all the weeds and plant positive new ideas in their place."

Louise L. Hay

Gardening is a wonderful hobby that both Kath and I treasure. It is a chance to be outside in the warmth with just the sounds of nature in the background. As I dig in the dirt, I am amazed each year to see the dreary grey winter landscape transform into rainbow walkways. Each day outdoors is another opportunity to perfect my own little masterpiece.

Like watering, weeding is a necessary chore in maintaining a garden. As the flowers or vegetables grow, the weeds need to be removed to keep the plants growing strong and healthy.

For today, focus on the thought that your personal struggles are just weeds.

Your negative issues can be removed from your thoughts. There is no reason to despise yourself for having problems that need to be dealt with. Remember, they are just weeds. Realize that you can work on them a little each day.

Like a garden, life is a step by step process.

Fill your mind with the beauty of what can be.

Keep working on it and create the masterpiece

You are meant to be.

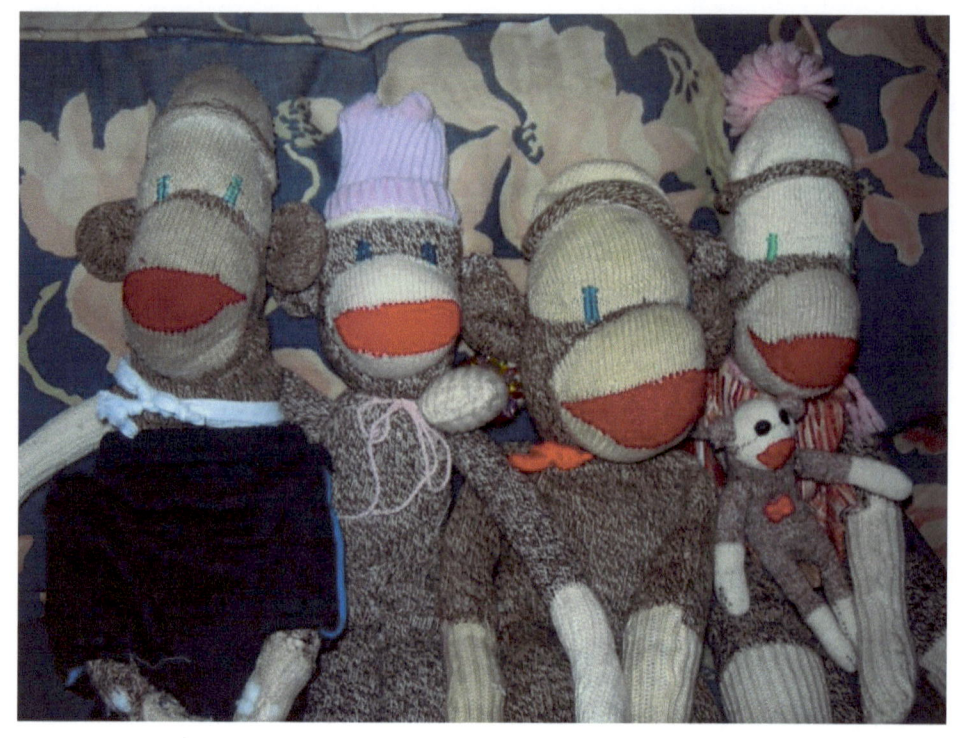

"The great man is he
who does not lose his child's heart."

Mencius

Children laugh out loud for no reason at all. They jump in puddles, and revel in the sound of leaves crunching under their feet.

They believe in magic and all kinds of imaginary beings. Children are born with hearts that love everyone and reach curiously to touch all that life offers.

Age teaches us to be cautious of the dangers of the world, and life demands that we become responsible.

But simple innocent joys will always make us smile because our own child's heart will always beat within us.

Today, give that child a chance to show through your very adult exterior.

-Skip to the car.

-Tickle someone you love.

-Tell a really dumb joke.

It's surprising how very good it feels.

Go ahead, be a monkey!

"Stop putting your life on hold.

Your best life is here- in this very moment.

You are ready- go for it."

Denise Marek

There are a few people I know who are angry all the time. They hold past hurts to them like old friends and hug their anger closely like a shield against the world. Instead of moving ahead in life they prefer to define themselves as victims and stay firmly rooted in a miserable past. No matter who is to blame or what terrible thing they may have done, none of us should choose to stay in such pain. Hate is such a heavy emotion. It drains all your energy and holds you locked in lonely darkness.

For today, say a prayer for the people you know trapped in anger and despair.

Wish for them the courage to jump back into life. Send them compassion and hope that they can find a way towards redemption. Sometimes if friends are by your side it makes it a lot easier to take that first scary leap. Leave that past behind and jump together in the now.

In this very moment your very best life is waiting for you. Go for it!

"Consciously cultivating thankfulness is a journey of the soul, one that begins when we look around us and see the positive effects that gratitude creates."

MJ Ryan

I volunteer at a soup kitchen and see firsthand how reciprocal kindness to others can be.

I see tired lost souls, sometimes dirty and often drunk or afflicted with mental illness, line up for a warm meal. It is such a contrast to the comfortable life I lead. I know I cannot eliminate hunger or change their circumstances, but I can hug and listen and share food with a few people.

My burdens lighten as I share theirs and we all come away feeling a little less alone, and grateful for the time we had together.

Try today to touch someone else's life, even if it is just eye contact, a smile, or a thank you to a stranger.

Look at life through their eyes. Look with compassion. Feel the connection we all have to one another.

Try to be consciously aware of how good your life is, and just

Say, Thank you.

"It is good to appreciate that life is now,
Whatever it offers, little or much,
Life is now, this day, this hour."

Charles Macomb Flandreau

It is magical and inspiring when you take the time to watch the sun come up. The colors and brightness slowly fill the sky and warm up the world for another day.

So beautiful- so precious and miraculous:

Watching the dawn is a much better start to the day than watching the latest litany of gossip, murder, and tragedy on television. Those images start your day with such a discouraging outlook. Why in the world do we watch this?

For today, don't watch the horror and don't listen to the terrible stories announced in the media.

Replace them with poetry or music or whatever inspires you.

Your approach to each day matters-

Practice appreciation,

Focus on the positive

Each moment of life is yours to mold and create.

Give this day,

This hour

Your loving attention.

"Happiness cannot be traveled to, owned, earned, won or consumed.

Happiness is a spiritual experience of living every minute with love, grace, and gratitude."

Denis Waitley

Through the years I have attended Methodist, Roman Catholic, Congregational and Unitarian Universalist services. I am a Reiki Master and I study holistic, pagan, Buddhist and earth centered practices. I have found pieces of myself in most of these spiritual beliefs. I have also discovered that more than any one particular theology, I believe in love.

Love is always the answer to my questions and struggles and it bursts from me like the pollen does from the center of this lily. The many pieces of my search for happiness are like the individual petals on the flower. Each is separate but they join in the center to complete a wonderful and joyous piece of beauty.

Today, I want you to realize that you are also a blessed and beautiful creation.

You are the composite of all your successes and failures. Each has served to help you grow. Each has been a part of creating the very special and unique being that you are.

Rejoice in it!

Be grateful for another day to continue to learn, to continue to find your spiritual contentment.

"It's our attitude in life that determines life's attitude toward us."

Earl Nightingad

Are you crabby?

Do you start out every day in an aggressive stance just waiting to be attacked?

Did you ever stop to think that maybe this approach will always put other people on the defense whenever you are near?

Just for today- smile and laugh

No Matter What.

Stuck in traffic?   Smile and laugh.

Be happy you have a car.

Surrounded by incompetence?   Smile and laugh.

The job will eventually get done.

No matter what-Smile and laugh.

And maybe, just maybe,

When you take time to look up-

Everyone around you

Is smiling and laughing too.

"He is a wise man who does not grieve for things which he has not, but rejoices for those which he has."

Epictus

Things- stuff- possessions- titles-

All the markers our society deems as signs of success or failure.

I've noticed that many of the people with the most "stuff" are terribly unhappy- never satisfied- always grabbing for more, and so fearful that someone will take what they have.

Focus today on what cannot be taken from you-

-The appreciation of the simple beauty of flowers clustered together in joy.

-The warmth of friends as we stumble through joys and sorrows together.

-Memories of children's laughter.

- The power of music to touch your soul.

There really is so much to rejoice in.

What are your treasures?

What has the most value in your life?

"Tenderness and kindness are not signs of weakness and despair, but manifestations of strength and resolution."

Khalil Gibran

Look at the branches in this photo. They are weighed down with the burden of the heavy wet snow, almost breaking. Yet they manage to bend with their load and can even be a place of rest for the winter birds. Life can feel like that kind of burden- holding you down. Your shoulders ache from too much responsibility. You feel the anger and frustration building. You just want to snap.

Today, instead of breaking, try to find a way to bend.

Look for ways to be tender and soothing to yourself. Reach out for assistance, that's what friends are for. We are communal by nature, and thrive when we help each other out. When the burdens are shared, they are never quite as hard to carry. Like the snow spread out across the bush, each little branch adds strength and carries a small amount of the total weight.

Just as the spring will eventually come and melt that heavy snow, your present worries will in time, be resolved.

"A mind at peace, a mind centered and not focused on harming others, is stronger than any physical force in the universe."

Wayne Dyer

Starfish are astonishing animals. They don't weigh very much, they are not very large and yet they survive as they cling to the rocks along the ocean. They ride out storms and tide all while battling other creatures trying to eat them! One of the most amazing facts of these tenacious beings is that they can regenerate an appendage when it has been lost. Some can even regenerate an entirely new sea star from just one remaining arm. Wow.

I have read stories of people who have survived terrible ordeals and tragedies and found ways to rebuild their lives. They were able to focus on a powerful reason to live and most times that purpose has been for love.

Today center your thoughts and focus on why you are alive.

What do you think your purpose is? What is it that you cling to? Who is it that you love? Take inspiration from the lowly starfish and know that you too are an incredibly powerful force in the universe.

"We are shaped by our thoughts;

We become what we think.

When the mind is pure, joy follows like a shadow that never leaves."

Siddhartha Gautama Buddha

There have been many times through the years that I have looked back at my life and been dismayed at some bad or cowardly decisions I have made. As a parent there is an abundance of could have, should have, but none of it can be changed. We all have both good and bad in ourselves. Like the shadows piercing through this wilderness picture both dark and light are simply parts of life's existence. Every day you have the opportunity to choose which one to follow.

If my thoughts are dark and angry my responses to others will match that. If my point of view is hopeful and based in love I know I will make better decisions: ones that I will be less likely to regret.

For today, choose to follow the path that is bright with light and joy.

Be expectant of the wonders that just might lie ahead. Anticipate happy outcomes to problems.

Trust yourself, and know that all will be well.

"The way we choose to respond when others make mistakes can cause them to feel ashamed or can allow them to remember our kindness and share our stories with future generations."

Michael Sedas

I was a chubby child and some people cruelly called me "Fatty Patty". I still cringe when I see pictures of myself looking so awkward and uncomfortable. The mockery made me feel ugly and the shame pushed me towards more eating to soothe my hurts. I did however have a very special uncle who always called me beautiful:

Always.

Uncle Jimmy struggled with weight issues too and he helped me to see that I was a lovely person, even if the exterior didn't always match that image. His gentle encouragement still inspires me to look for what is beautiful in me and others.

For today, be aware of what you say and how it is said.

People make mistakes. It is part of being human. Your response can encourage them to strive to do better next time. Your kindness can start a ripple of good deeds from that one person to many others.

Your gentle hand can help lead someone else to a bright and happy future.

"Life is like a mirror.

We get the best results when we smile at it."

Unknown

My husband and I took a trip to Italy and stayed at a villa in Tuscany. Despite dark clouds and a chilly wind, we decided one morning to hike the nearby olive grove. We ended up getting caught in a rain shower and started to run back to the villa figuring our adventure was a bust. However, we came across an ancient chapel tucked in the hillside and found shelter on old stone benches under the archway. We watched the rain water the olive trees as fog misted over the valley. It was haunting and magically beautiful. The ruined adventure became a romantic and treasured memory.

Today choose to smile at the rainstorms that may come your way. Let your reflection be bright and optimistic.

The lake in this picture reflects the allure of the colors of the American southwest. The beauty is enhanced as the image is duplicated in the water. In the same way your smile can enhance your beauty and brighten your outlook on the day ahead.

Let your smile show a willingness to be joyful.

Let your smile be the mirror that reflects and magnifies the best in you.

"Try not to become a person of success,

But rather try to become a person of value."

Albert Einstein

Lying has become a national epidemic. Bankers, politicians, educators and clergy ensnared in cover-ups and scandals that dishonor the positions of authority that they are in. Like insects caught in a spider web they thrash away trying to deny and escape from the situation they put themselves into.

We watch in horror, enraged at their evil- as we should. Truth and integrity matter. Decency and honesty should always be what we strive for. Their errors are so large- so clear to see. In comparison, the small lies in life are easy to ignore.

Is it okay to lie to take a day off from work or to make up a story to cover up a mistake you made? No matter the size of an untruth, it still dishonors the value of a truly successful human being.

Today choose to be a person of courage and integrity.

Speak only truth to yourself and others.

Let your reflection in life be honest and clear.

Let your image be worthy of the person you aspire to be.

"All the art of living lies in a fine mingling of

letting go and holding on."

Havelock Ellis

Living near the ocean has given me the opportunity to see the power and rhythm of the tides. There is a continual cycle of high and low water crashing or gliding onto the beach.

Nothing can stop it and we shouldn't try to. It is part of the rhythm of the life of this planet.

The high tides bring pounding and sometimes destructive waves to our coast. I know they will in time cease- to lead into the time of soft bubbles washing over what remains.

Today- send blessings to the storms you have weathered, and let them go.

They are in the past and it is time to leave them there.

The cycle of life-

The heartbeat of creation-

Hold on-

Let go-

Find your rhythm.

"We must be willing to let go of the life we planned,

So as to accept the life that is waiting for us."

Joseph Campbell

In my high school yearbook I wrote that I wanted to be a psychologist. Instead I ended up quitting college, marrying very young, and had 3 children by the time I was 28.

Years went by- they grew- and so did I. Eventually I had a successful business career, but I found happiness-

-With my family- sharing daily problems and joys.

-At the soup kitchen - listening.

-Expressing my thoughts as I write this book.

I am not the psychologist as I had planned but, in retrospect, it has been quite a full and happy life helping and caring for people I love.

Today- Let go of the controls.

Take a moment and think about the things in your life that bring you joy. They are the best indicators of the wonderful life waiting for you,

Or maybe already there.

Focus your energies on that joy, that light.

Feel it calling to you, and accept it.

"When you look for the bad in mankind expecting to find it, you surely will."

Pollyanna,
Eleanor H. Porter

This is a close-up of a dandelion puff. Dandelions: those irritating weeds that mess up a perfect green lawn and just won't die. You know the puffs that float through the air and cover your car's windshield with pollen. This is the creator of that airborne dust that makes you sneeze and turns your nose red. Dandelions are such an annoyance aren't they?

Or is there another way to view it?

Today, try being a Pollyanna and instead of looking at the bad, look for the good instead.

You will see one of Mother Nature's marvelous creations. It is a perfect circle spinning in the warm air, almost like a tiny Ferris wheel. It looks so delicate, yet you know it is quite tenacious.

This little puff will send seeds into the air to find a place to grow. It is part of the creation of bright yellow flowers that dot the landscape- Flowers that are just the right size for tiny fingers to pick.

Look closely and see a bright bouquet of smiles- just for you.

It is only a matter of perception.

"Dare to live the life you have dreamed for yourself.

Go forward and make your dreams come true."

Ralph Waldo Emerson

"I dare you!" How many times did childhood friends say that to you, pushing you to do something extreme? Sometimes those dares got you into trouble when you took the prize peonies from the neighbor's yard or tried to fly off your grandfather's garage. Childish dares did tend to prove to be bad decisions, but the exhilaration you felt was sometimes worth it. Remember the thrill of those wild adventures?

What wild adventure is still there inside you waiting for you to chase it? Does this walkway beckon you to find where it leads? Would you like to put yourself into this photograph and follow it to the other side of those trees?

For today, go ahead and let a friend push you into the extreme.

Be willing to take a chance.

Step onto this footpath and follow it into the unknown. You may find it leads exactly where you always wanted to be.

Go ahead- I dare you!

61.

"The final forming of a person's character lies in their own hands."

Anne Frank

Crocheting is a relaxing pastime for me. My busy fingers keep me from mindless snacking and I make warm blankets for family and friends. If I make a mistake I can just pull it out and redo it. The finished result follows the exact pattern and is symmetrical and color coordinated. Life doesn't follow a set pattern and is a kaleidoscope of changing colors. Every day presents new challenges and goals seem to change every few years. Like the crocheted afghan though, it is all up to me as to what the results will be.

> I choose to be happy or sad.
>
> I choose to be alone or in a circle of friends.
>
> I choose the pattern of my life.

Today, be clear on what you choose to do.

You cannot control what life will send your way, but you can choose how you respond to it. Anne Frank was able to choose a life of love in the midst of evil. Amazing.

Whatever comes your way today, choose a positive and gentle response.

> Make a life of gentle courage,
>
> A life you are proud of.

"Promise me you'll always remember:

You're braver than you believe,

And stronger than you seem,

And smarter than you think."

Christopher Robin to Pooh Bear

A.A. Milne

The best children's books were written for both the little ones listening and the adults reading them aloud. Children hear the story. We see the subtle messages.

Pooh Bear and butterflies are two of my favorite creatures. To me, they exemplify innocence and hope. Because of that strong combination in my own life, I partner them for my last message to you dear friend.

Pooh lives in the beginning stage of knowledge and wonder, forever innocent.

Butterflies go through many stages before becoming what they were meant to be: ugly worm, dormant cocoon, and finally miraculous beauty.

No matter what stage you are in right now, let the butterfly give you hope.

Today,

Take a good look in the mirror at yourself
See who you really are,
Beautiful- Growing- Changing
Learning- Strong- Brave,

And Forever Hopeful.
Promise me that you'll always remember that.
Blessings,

Patti

About the Author

Patti lives with her husband, her dog Maggie and a cat named Oz on a small pond in a rural New England town. Days are filled with caring for her grandson, her gardens, practicing Reiki, and volunteer work at a local soup kitchen, a homeless shelter and Habitat for Humanity. The heart of Patti's life is with her family and friends. Every day is a treasure to dive into with smiles. Each day is another opportunity to grow and learn.

About the Photographer

Completing this book has fulfilled the first step in one of Kathleen's life dreams: to heal the earth with her photography and vibrational therapy. She sees and feels the beauty of the earth and captures the moment and the presence of the divine. Immersing oneself in the photo we are drawn out of the continual thinking state into a positive feeling state. Doing this makes it possible to heal your life.

Kalein Crystal Bowl Therapy is Kathleen's business on Cape Cod where she lives with her husband.

www.ingramcontent.com/pod-product-compliance
Lightning Source LLC
Chambersburg PA
CBHW042333150426
43194CB00001B/40